The Best Bunny

The Adventures of lil Shen
(and her inspirational sidekick, Bunny Best)

written by
Shenandoah Chefalo

illustrated by
Alena Tkach

My name is Lil Shen.
And this silly thing is Bunny Best.
Sometimes I just call them Bunny B.

I want to tell you about one of my worst days.
It was the day of my grandma's funeral, and I was very sad.

But it was also the first day
I met my lovely Bunny B.

"Are you ready to go, Lil Shen?"

Lil Shen looked down at her shoes.
They were black and shiny.
She spent ages polishing them, to get them just right.
"Yes, Muriel," she called. "I'm ready."

But she wasn't really ready.
She didn't want to go at all.
Not to this.
Not to Grandma's funeral.

Lil Shen imagined what it would be like.

Would she have to look inside the casket?

Would she have to talk to people?
Would she be allowed to cry?

Muriel waited in the car.
Her hand tapped impatiently on the steering wheel.
Lil Shen bundled into the back and closed the door.
There was a small, wrapped package on the seat next to her.

"That's for you," said Muriel, and she started the car.
"But don't open it until later."
Lil Shen stared at the parcel. What was inside?

This day was the worst.
Lil Shen stood at the back of the room.
She didn't look inside the casket –
she hadn't even been asked.
She didn't talk to people –
no one even noticed she was there.

And she didn't cry. Not there. Not on her own.

It was raining when they got home.
Muriel passed Lil Shen the package from the car.
"It's from your grandma," she said.
Lil Shen ran upstairs and closed the door.

She curled up on her bed
and tore open the wrapper.

"Hi!"
A small, soft, fluffy, rabbit toy fell onto the bed
from the parcel and smiled up at Lil Shen.
"I'm Bunny Best!"

Lil Shen looked right at Bunny Best. Her eyes were wide.
"You can talk?"

Bunny Best twitched their ears.
"Yup!"
"But how?"

Lil Shen put the stuffy down onto her pillow.
"And why?"

"I don't know," said Bunny Best. "But isn't it great?"

Lil Shen peered at them. "I think it's because of my Imagine-A-Shen," she said.

Lil Shen's grandma had always laughed about that.
"You're good at seeing things
that not everyone can see," she had said.
"I think it's because of your Imagine-A-Shen."
"My what?" Lil Shen asked.

Grandma took her hand.
"Other people have simple imaginations, but you are Lil Shen."
"You don't just have an imagination,
you have a special, super-powered..."
"IMAGINE-A-SHEN!"

Lil Shen put Bunny Best on her knee.
"Grandma always says
I can solve any problem with my Imagine-A-Shen."
"Sounds great," said Bunny B.

"Do you have anything I can eat?"

Lil Shen pulled a cupcake
out of her pocket.
It was a little squashed.

"You can have this.
I took it from the funeral."

Lil Shen began to cry.
Bunny Best put the cupcake down.
They wrapped their small bunny arms around Lil Shen's knee.
"It's OK. You cry. You cry just as much as you need."

While Bunny Best ate the cupcake and the rain hammered at the window, Lil Shen thought of her grandma.

She remembered how Grandma loved to cook.

She remembered how Grandma loved to sew.

She remembered how Grandma did puzzles.

he remembered Grandma pushing her on the swing.

She remembered Grandma playing dollies with her.

She remembered Grandma.

It became dark.
"Do you feel better?" Bunny Best asked.
"A little."
"It will take time. You won't feel better right away."
"Did you eat all of the cupcake?"
"No, I saved a little for you."

Lil Shen woke up in the morning.
She forgot to clean her teeth!

"I'll just be a minute, Grandma," she called,
rushing to the bathroom.
But Grandma wasn't there. Just Muriel.

"I'm coming, Muriel. I won't be long."

Lil Shen slumped onto her bed.
"I can't do it, Bunny," she said. "I can't pretend to be OK."
"Then don't." Bunny B hopped over to her.
"Just always do your best."
"Bunny Best," said Lil Shen. "The best bunny!"

Lil Shen did her best.
She got dressed.

She ate her breakfast.

She packed her things
into her backpack,
including Bunny B.

And she went to school.

It got easier.

Lil Shen still missed
her grandma.
But she did her best,
and eventually, she felt OK.

"You know what?"
Bunny Best asked, a few weeks later.
"What?"
"I think we should have some adventures.
Have I told you about my friends?"
Lil Shen smiled. "No. What friends?"

www.ingramcontent.com/pod-product-compliance
Lightning Source LLC
LaVergne TN
LVRC081530230625
813831LV00022B/36